WILD FOOD
RECIPES

compiled by
Simon Haseltine

*Illustrated with nostalgic
pastoral scenes
of country life*

SALMON

Index

Cover pictures *front:* "Blackberry Time" by Myles Birket Foster
back: "The Gleaners" by Myles Birket Foster
Title page: "Spring" by Frederick Walker

Printed and Published by J. Salmon Ltd., Sevenoaks, England © Copyright

Tips on foraging for wild food

Whether you are a wonderful family cook, love exploring the great outdoors, or simply enjoy strolling in your local inner city park, foraging for your own meals is something we can all do. The definition of foraging is 'the act of looking for, or searching for food and provisions', and relates to anything that we can find growing in the wild. This book concentrates on edible wild nuts and plants for you to gather, but there are many fungi, animals, fish and crustacean waiting for you to discover as your experience and knowledge grows. And, of course, many of the wild foods we find are the ancestor of our modern cultivated crops, so by gathering and eating them, we are also enjoying the family menus, tastes and cooking smells of our own ancestors.

Wild food has no packaging, food miles, sprays or chemicals, so to fully enjoy nature at its very best, always be careful where you pick to avoid any contamination. Polluted areas like roadsides, animal tracks and intensively farmed field edges should be avoided and always wash your food when you get home. Land access laws are complex and vary across the UK, so check with the landowner before you enter private land and the bye laws covering public land. Remember, don't pick if you are uncertain of what you have found, so it is a good idea to take a handy guide with you to identify edible plants. Start with picking a few dandelions, wild garlic and nettles to make a tasty supper and, as your confidence grows, foraging courses are available to further your knowledge before you gather more exotic plants, fungi or crustacean. Your wild food culinary skills and taste buds will soon develop so you can enjoy nature's free and bountiful larder.

Wild Mushroom and Nettle Lasagne

Best using fresh young springtime nettles – and don't forget to wear gloves!

Nettles, enough to fill around 1 to 2 plastic shopping bags   1 tin chopped tomatoes
1 onion (chopped)   Handful wild garlic (chopped)   Juice of 1 lemon
Lasagne sheets   Small tub crème fraiche   8 oz. Cheddar cheese (grated)
Small red chilli (chopped)   Salt, pepper, nutmeg   A little milk, flour, butter

Rinse the nettles well, remove the stalks and chop roughly. In a large pan, melt a knob of butter with a drizzle of olive oil and sauté the garlic for a minute or so then add the nettles and fry lightly for a further 2 minutes until they wilt (like spinach). Next, add the lemon juice and salt, pepper and nutmeg, cover the pan and simmer gently for a further 5 minutes, tossing occasionally. Stir in the crème fraiche. In the meantime, make a basic tomato sauce by sautéing the onion and chilli in a little oil for 5 minutes or until soft, then add the chopped tomatoes and reduce slowly for around 5 minutes. For the béchamel sauce, add 1 heaped dessertspoon of flour to a knob of melted butter in a saucepan and mix to a paste. Gradually stir in enough milk until you have a thick white sauce. Fold in three quarters of the grated cheese and stir in until melted. Build up lasagne in a baking dish by alternating layers of lasagne sheets, nettles and tomato sauce. Finish with a layer of lasagne sheets and pour the béchamel sauce over top and sprinkle over the remaining cheese. Cook in a preheated oven at Gas mark 6/200C° for around 30 minutes or until golden brown.

Rabbit and Crab Apple Stew with Wild Herb Dumplings

A wild hearty stew...

1 medium rabbit (jointed)   4 crab apples (peeled and chopped)
2 onions (chopped)   2 bay leaves   Black pepper to taste
Sprig fresh seasonal herbs   4 carrots (peeled and chunked)
4 potatoes (peeled and chunked)

Dumplings:
1 cup flour   ½ cup suet   Salt and pepper to taste
Handful wild garlic leaves (finely chopped)
2 tsps baking powder   1 cup cold water

Place the prepared rabbit into large casserole dish or slow cooker, add the onions, bay leaves, carrots, potatoes, black pepper and herbs and just cover with water. Place in the oven and cook gently at Gas 4/180C° for 2 hours. Meanwhile, make the dumplings by combining the flour, suet, seasoning, baking powder and garlic in a mixing bowl and add water to form a soft dough. Divide the dough into 8 small balls and gently drop into the casserole together with the apple pieces and cook for a further 30 minutes. Serves 4.

Nettle Curry

Delicious served with Dandelion Bhaji…

5 handfuls of fresh nettles (washed to remove bugs)   6 potatoes (peeled and chopped)
2 onions (chopped)   1 handful wild garlic (chopped)   ½ tbsp grated ginger
4 tsp curry powder   1 red chilli (chopped)   Salt   Oil

In a large pan, bring the potatoes to a boil and simmer until tender. Meanwhile, place the curry powder, onions, wild garlic, chilli and ginger in a frying pan with a little oil and sauté for around 5 minutes until soft. Next, add the nettles and ½ cup potato water to the onion mixture and cook for a further 5 minutes. Cool slightly and purée. Drain the potatoes and return to the pan with ½ cup of water. Fold in the onion and nettle purée and simmer gently for 10 minutes to thicken. Add salt to taste. Serves 4 with the Dandelion Bhaji.

Dandelion Bhaji

30 dandelion heads, all stalks removed   1 onion (chopped)
Handful wild celery (chopped)   1 tsp. curry powder   4 oz. flour   2 eggs   Oil

Beat the eggs in a bowl and add the onions and dandelion heads and mix well. Stir in the flour, wild celery and curry powder and combine. Heat the oil in a deep-sided frying pan over a medium heat. When hot add a large spoonful of the bhaji mixture and fry for around a minute until golden-brown, turning once. Remove and drain on kitchen paper. Serves 4 as an accompaniment to your favourite curry.

Wild Mushroom Risotto

A risotto with a wild twist…

2 handfuls of nettle tips
1 small handful of sorrel leaves (chopped)
1 small handful wild celery (chopped)
1 small handful wild garlic leaves (chopped)
1 onion   Large handful wild mushrooms (sliced)
1 pt vegetable stock (hot)   1lb risotto rice
2 oz cheese (grated)   1 oz butter
Salt and pepper to taste

Sauté the onion for 5 minutes and wash the nettles to remove any bugs. Add the nettles and mushrooms to the onion and gently fry for 5 further minutes or until the nettles have wilted. Sprinkle the risotto rice over the onion mixture, then start to add the stock, a little at a time. Gently simmer until the stock has been absorbed. Just a few minutes before cooking has finished, add the chopped herbs, grated cheese and butter, and season to taste. Serves 2.

Elderberry Syrup

A rich, delicious syrup…

2 lbs. elderberries
Sugar
Water
Pinch spices (try cloves or cinnamon)

Wash and weigh the elderberries and place in a large saucepan. Add the spices and mash roughly with a potato masher to break their skins. Weigh out the same amount of sugar and add that to the saucepan. Just cover the berries and sugar with water and bring to the boil, simmer gently for 20 minutes, then strain through a sieve. Use immediately, or store in sterilised bottles in the fridge. Dilute to make a cordial or pour over desserts.

Hedgerow Wine

Your own label red wine and not a penny in tax to pay…

**2 lbs. blackberries   1 lb. elderberries   2 ripe bananas   2 Campden tablets
3 lbs. sugar   1 sachet wine yeast   1 sachet nutrient   Water**

Wash the elderberries and blackberries to remove any bugs. Put the fruit into a fermenting bin and crush with a clean potato masher and pour over 4 pints of water. Dissolve 1 Campden tablet in a little warm water and add to the fruit. Next, boil half of the sugar in 2 pints of water for 2 minutes and cool before stirring into the fruit. Peel and squash the bananas and add to the fruit. Finally, add the yeast and nutrient and cover and allow to ferment for a week, stirring daily.

After a week, strain the mixture and return the juice to a clean fermenting bin. Boil the rest of the sugar in 1 pint of water for 2 minutes and cool before adding to the juice. Cover again and leave for a further 4 days. Then pour the juice into a glass gallon jar, leaving behind as much deposit as possible. Top up with cooled, boiled water to where the neck begins, fit a fermentation lock, and leave until fermentation has finished. Rack into a second fermentation jar, adding 1 crushed Campden tablet to help clear the wine. Once clear, siphon into sterilised bottles, cork and ready to drink after a month or so.

Seaweed Flan

A taste of the seaside on your plate…

6 oz. plain flour	1 egg (beaten)
½ tsp. salt	4 fl. oz. milk
Cold water (around 3 fl. oz.)	2 oz. cheese (grated)
3 oz. margarine	2 oz. seaweed (shredded)
2 tsp. cornflour	Salt and pepper to taste

Rub margarine into flour using your fingers until the mixture resembles breadcrumbs. Add salt and gradually stir in the cold water and mix to a very stiff, smooth pastry. Rest the pastry in the fridge for 30 minutes, then roll out and line a greased 6 inch flan tin or deep pie plate. Bake blind for 10 minutes at 200C°/Gas 6. Meanwhile, mix the cornflour with the egg in a bowl, add the milk, seaweed and cheese. Season to taste then pour into baked flan case and sprinkle with cheese. Bake for 20 minutes at Gas 6/200C° until set and golden brown. Serve hot or cold. Serves 4.

Sea Veg Stew

A warming seaside stew with a hint of wild garlic…

1 lb. selection of seasonal vegetables *(try carrot, potato, onion, turnip, leeks)*
4 oz. kelp seaweed   Handful wild garlic leaves
Handful wild celery   2 knobs butter
Vegetable stock (around 1 pt – enough to cover)
Pinch dried herbs   1 tin crushed tomatoes

Wash and soak the kelp seaweed in fresh water for 10 min. Meanwhile, chop the vegetables into bite-size pieces and chop the herbs. Place the kelp, herbs, tomatoes and prepared vegetables into a stew pan, add the dried herbs and season to taste. Dot with butter, then add the stock to just cover the vegetables. Cook gently on the hob for around an hour, or until the vegetables are tender. Serve with a jacket potato. Serves 4.

Salty Seaweed Soup

A taste of the seaside…

Handful dulse seaweed
Handful channel wrack kelp seaweed
1 lb. potatoes (peeled and chopped)
2 onions (chopped)
Handful wild garlic (chopped)
Water (to cover)
Pepper

Add potatoes and onions to a large pot and just cover with water. Bring to the boil and simmer for 20 minutes or until tender adding the wild garlic. Rinse and chop the seaweed and add to the soup and simmer for a further 10 minutes. Serves 4 with chunky bread.

Rose Hip Crumble

A fruity hedgerow crumble

Short crust pastry (enough for single-crust 9 inch pie dish)
1 cup dried rose hips   2 fl. oz. milk
6 oz. plain flour (sifted)   2 tsp. baking powder
Pinch salt   4 oz. margarine   6 oz. brown sugar
2 egg yolks (beaten)   2 egg whites
Handful wild walnuts (chopped) or any wild nuts

Wash the rose hips and remove stems and any flower remnants. Soften by gently simmering in milk for 20 minutes, then leave to cool. Meanwhile, sift together the flour, baking powder and salt. Cream the margarine and brown sugar until the mixture has a crumbly texture. Reserve half the crumble for the topping and add the egg yolks, milk and rose hips to the remainder. Beat the egg whites until stiff peaks and fold into the berry mixture. Spoon into a pie dish and sprinkle with the remaining crumble topping. Garnish with the walnuts and bake (Gas 6/200C°) for 40 minutes or until the crumble is golden brown. Serves 6 with custard or ice cream.

Happy Moments
by Henry John Sylvester Stannard

Mussels with a Samphire and Wild Garlic Sauce

A taste of the sea...

4 lbs. mussels
1 handful wild garlic leaves (shredded)
1 onion (chopped)
1 large handful samphire
Large knob butter
3½ fl. oz. dry white wine or cider
4 fl. oz. double cream
Handful of wild celery (coarsely chopped)

Wash the prepared mussels under plenty of cold, running water and discard any open ones that won't close when lightly squeezed. Sauté the onion, samphire and garlic leaves in the butter in a large pan for around 5 minutes. Add the mussels and wine, turn up the heat, cover and steam for 4 minutes, giving the pan a good shake every minute or so. Fold in the cream and chopped celery leaves and remove from the heat. Serve with hunks of warm crusty bread. Serves 4.

Wild Walnut and Apple Pie

A delicious old fashion apple pie…

Short crust pastry (enough for double-crust 9 inch pie dish)
4 oz. sugar   2 tbsps. flour   ¼ tsp. cinnamon
Pinch salt   1 tsp. orange peel (grated)   ½ cup honey
1 large knob of butter   12 oz. fresh cranberries
1 lb. crab apples (peeled, cored and diced)
3 oz. wild walnuts   1 egg (beaten)

Melt the butter and add the sugar, flour, cinnamon, salt, orange peel, honey and cook gently for around 2 minutes, stirring all the time. Next add the cranberries, diced apples and walnuts and cook for a further 5 minutes until the fruit has softened. Divide the pastry and line a pie dish. Spoon the filling onto the pie base and cover with the remaining pastry. Brush the crust with egg wash and bake in a hot oven (Gas 6/200C°) for 40 minutes or until golden brown. Serve with custard. Serves 4.

Tangy Crab Apple Jelly

A delicious tangy jelly to accompany roast pork…

3 lbs. crab apples (chopped)
2 lbs. sugar (approx)
Water

Place the chopped crab apples in a pan and cover with water. Cook the apples gently for around 10 minutes or so until they are a soft pulp. Strain the stewed apples through linen tea towel into a bowl, cover and leave overnight. The next day, add the sugar in the ratio of 1 pint of juice for each 1 lb. of sugar. Boil in a large pan until the mixture reaches setting point, then pour into sterilised jars and seal immediately. Serve with roast pork or cold meats.

Rose Hip Syrup

An autumn treat that's good for you, full of vitamin C...

4 cups rose hips
2 cups water
1 cup sugar

Wash the rose hips and remove stems and any flower remnants. Gently simmer the rose hips in the water for 20 minutes in a covered saucepan. Strain through a jelly bag and return the clear juice to the pan, adding the sugar. Stir well and boil for a further five minutes. Bottle into warm sterilised jars and refrigerate. Serve over ice cream, or delicious over your breakfast muesli.

Spicy Crab Apply Chutney

Delicious in a ham sandwich…

1½ lbs. crab apples (peeled, cored and chopped)
8 oz. brown sugar   1 onion
2 tsps. turmeric   ½ pt cider vinegar
1 chilli pepper (chopped)   Pinch salt
¼ inch fresh ginger (grated)

Place the prepared apples in a heavy-based saucepan and stir in all other ingredients, cover and bring to the boil. Reduce heat to low and gently simmer for at least an hour, stirring occasionally. Once the liquid has all evaporated and the chutney has thickened, remove from heat and pour into sterilised jars, stir chutney, seal and label. Serve with cold meats. Makes around 2 lbs. of chutney.

Mulberry Jam

A taste of summer…

Equal weights mulberries and sugar
Juice of one lemon for every lb of fruit
Wild fennel seeds

Heat the mulberries, sugar and lemon juice until gently simmering. Add the fennel seeds and continue simmering until setting point has been reached. Skim any froth from the surface and pot immediately into sterilised jars and seal. Makes approximately equal weight of jam to fruit used.

The High Grasses
by Edward Stott

Wild Nettle and Garlic Soup

Pick the nettles carefully…

1 lb. young nettle tops (washed)
1 leek (chopped)
1 onion (chopped)
Handful wild celery (chopped)
2 large potatoes (peeled and chopped)

Handful wild garlic leaves (shredded)
1 pint vegetable stock
Small tub single cream
Salt and pepper to taste
Oil

Mustard leaves (for garnish)

Place all ingredients in a large saucepan with water, except the cream and the mustard leaves, and bring to the boil. Simmer gently for 20 minutes or until the potatoes are tender, then cool and purée in a blender. Stir in the cream and reheat when required and garnish with the mustard leaves. Serves 4.

Chilled Crab Apple Soup

A spicy, tangy, chilled soup sensation…

12 crab apples (peeled and diced)
2 tbsps. of canola oil (or other neutral-tasting oil)
1 onion (diced)
Handful wild celery – chopped
½ tsp. curry powder of your choice
1 small chilli pepper (seeds removed and chopped)
1 lemon (juice only)
1 pt vegetable stock
Salt and pepper to taste

Sauté the onion and celery for a round 5 minutes, then add the chilli, apple and curry powder and stir for a further 5 minutes or until the apple softens. Add the stock and simmer for 40 minutes.

Allow soup to cool, then add lemon juice and season to taste. Purée in a blender and chill before serving. Serves 4.

Bread and Butter Pudding with Wild Berries

Blackberries freeze well, so a comfort pudding for a wild winter's evening…

10 slices white bread (crusts removed)	**½ tsp. ground cinnamon**
2 eggs (whisked)	**½ tsp. ground nutmeg**
1 pt milk	**6 oz. sugar**
2 oz. butter (plus a little for greasing)	**4 oz. blackberries**

Sprinkle the blackberries with 2 oz. sugar and leave in a bowl for a few minutes. Meanwhile, heat the milk with the cinnamon and nutmeg until just boiling, then stir in the eggs, butter and 4 oz. of the sugar and simmer for a few minutes. Butter a baking dish and layer the bread and blackberries, finishing with a layer of bread. Pour over the custard mixture and leave to absorb for 20 minutes or so. Cook in a preheated oven at Gas 6/200C° for 40 minutes or until brown and the custard has set. Serve hot with lashings of custard. Serves 4.

Gathering Flowers
by Myles Birket Foster

Strawberry Fool

Fancy something wild and fruity…

1 lb. wild strawberries
¼ cup caster sugar
½ cup mascarpone cheese
1 tsp. vanilla essence
1 egg white

Hull and slice the strawberries but keep 4 whole fruits aside. Combine the sliced strawberries with 1 tablespoon of caster sugar in a small pan and cook over a medium heat for 5 minutes until the fruit softens. Remove from the heat and place in a bowl to cool. Meanwhile, gently whisk the mascarpone and vanilla essence in a mixing bowl. Whisk the egg white in a separate bowl until soft peaks form. Gradually whisk the remaining caster sugar into the egg whites until they become thick and glossy. Gently fold the mascarpone into the egg white mixture with a large metal spoon, then fold in the cooled strawberry mixture. Divide the strawberry fool between 4 sundae glasses and decorate with the remaining strawberries. Serves 4.

Wild Blackberry Ice Cream

A great way to preserve your blackberry harvest…

8 fl. oz. double cream	**6 oz. caster sugar**
4 fl. oz. buttermilk	**1 lb. blackberries**
2 egg yolks	**1 tbsp. granulated sugar**

1 tsp. lemon juice

Gently heat the cream and buttermilk in a pan to just below simmering. Whisk the egg yolks with the caster sugar, then add to the hot milk and cream and cook gently over a low heat until the mixture thickens. Sieve into a tub and allow to cool. Meanwhile, heat the blackberries with the granulated sugar for a round 5 minutes or until the fruit softens, then whizz in blender and sieve out the pips. Fold the fruit purée into the cream mixture and churn or freeze until thick. Serves 6.

Bramble Jelly

My nan's favourite recipe…

3 lb. blackberries
4 crab apples (peeled, cored and chopped)
¾ pt water
1 lemon (juice only)
Granulated sugar

Put the blackberries, apples, water and lemon juice in a large pan and bring to the boil, then simmer gently for 25 minutes or until the fruit is soft. Place a linen tea towel over an upturned stool with a large bowl underneath, then tip the stewed fruit into the bag and leave to drip overnight. Measure the juice into a large pan and for every 1 pint, add 1 lb. sugar. Heat gently until the sugar has dissolved, stirring all the time, then bring to the boil and simmer for 10 minutes before you check if setting point has been reached. Skim away any scum, then pour into sterilised jam jars, cover and seal immediately. Makes around 4 jars.

Saturday Afternoon
by William Gunning King

Mushroom Soup

A foraged lunch...

2 leeks (chopped)	**8 oz. wild mushrooms (sliced)**
Large handful wild garlic (chopped)	**Small handful fresh herbs**
2 oz. butter	**1 pt. vegetable stock**

Simmer the leaks and garlic in the butter for around 5 minutes or until they are softened, then add the sliced mushrooms and herbs and cook for a further 5 minutes. Add the vegetable stock and simmer for a further 5 minutes. Blend in a food processor until smooth and serve hot with a chunk of freshly baked herby bread.

Autumn Chestnut, Hazelnut and Walnut Soup

A truly nutty soup…

1 lb. mixed wild nuts (sweet chestnuts, walnuts and hazelnuts)
Vegetable stock (to just cover)
2 bay leaves
½ tsp. of vanilla powder
1 small tub double cream

Prick the chestnuts, then boil for 10 minutes or until tender. Cool and peel. Place the shelled walnuts, hazelnuts and chestnuts on a baking tray and roast in a hot oven (Gas 7/220C°) for 15 minutes. Place the nuts in a pan and add the stock, bay leaves and vanilla powder and simmer for 20 minutes.

Cool slightly and blend in a food processor. Add the cream and heat gently before serving. Serves 4.

Nipplewort Pasta

A rich, cheesy pasta recipe…

Handful nipplewort greens (chopped)
Handful alexanders stems (chopped)
Small handful wild garlic (chopped)
Small handful wild celery (chopped)
Dried pasta (enough for 4 servings)
Tub crème fraiche   6 oz. Stilton cheese
2 leeks (thinly sliced)
3 tbsps. Dijon mustard or wholegrain mustard
Small jar sun-dried tomatoes
A little oil and knob of butter
Black pepper (to taste)

Add the leeks to the oil and butter in a large pan and sauté for 10 minutes or until soft. In a saucepan, boil the alexanders stems for 5 minutes, strain and add to the softened leeks, together with the Stilton, crème fraiche, mustard and black pepper and stir until the cheese has melted. Add the chopped herbs and cook for a further minute or so until the leaves have wilted. Meanwhile, boil the pasta according to the instructions on the packet, then drain and fold into sauce. Add the sun-dried tomatoes, stir and serve. Serves 3.

Blackberry Pancakes

Mouth watering pancakes…

4 oz. flour	8 fl. oz. whole milk
Pinch salt	1 tsp. vanilla extract
1 large egg (beaten)	4 oz. unsalted butter (melted)
2 tbsps. sugar	1 cup blackberries

Homemade blackberry ice cream

Sift together the flour and salt into a large mixing bowl. In a small bowl, add the egg, sugar, milk, vanilla and 2 oz. melted butter. Next, add the liquid to the flour mixture and stir until the batter has the consistency of thick cream.

Heat a large frying pan, add some of the remaining melted butter and gently dollop the batter into the pan to form small pancakes. Press a few blackberries into each pancake and cook for a minute or two until the undersides are golden brown and bubbles are breaking on top. Turn and cook 1 minute on the other side. Keep the cooked pancakes warm in the oven. Delicious served with homemade blackberry ice cream. Serves 4.

Lemon Balm and Garlic Pesto

Easy to make and so tasty…

Handful of lemon balm leaves
Small handful of wild garlic leaves
Handful wild celery
A few wild walnuts (shelled)
Olive oil
Salt (to taste)

Wash the leaves and then add all the ingredients into a blender with an egg cup of olive oil. Blend for a few moments, adding a little extra oil to form the required consistency. To serve, fold through drained cooked pasta.

Sorrel Omelette

A wild twist to the humble omelette…

4 eggs
Large knob butter
A little milk
Handful sorrel leaves (chopped)
Salt and pepper to taste

Break the eggs into a small bowl and whisk with a fork. Add a little milk, salt and pepper and mix well. Melt a little butter in an omelette pan (or small frying pan) and add half the sorrel leaves and cook for a minute or two until wilted. Next, pour half the egg mixture in and continue cooking over a medium heat for around 5 minutes until the egg has set. Keep the omelette warm and repeat for the remaining egg mixture. Serve with a salad.

In the Meadow
by Edward Wilkins Waite

F W WAITE

Nettle Beer

A distinguished and refreshing hedgerow beer…

Around 2 lbs. nettle tops (top 6 leaves and stalk)
1 gallon water
1 lb. demerara sugar
2 lemons (peeled and juice)
1 oz. cream of tartar
½ oz. brewers yeast

Gently wash and drain the nettles, ensuring they are free of bugs. Place the nettles into the water in a large pan and boil for 20 minutes, or until the nettles are well cooked. Strain the liquid into a large container and discard the nettles. Add the sugar, lemon rind and juice and cream of tartar, stir well. Allow to cool to about 21°C (70°F), then remove a little of the liquid and mix with the yeast, stir the yeast mixture back into the liquid. Cover the container with a clean cloth and leave in a warm place for 3 days. Strain the ale into sterilised bottles, cap with crown caps (using a bottle capping gadget) and leave for at least a week to clear before drinking.

Nettle Tea

A mild and refreshing cuppa…

1 tbsp. dried nettle leaves (per person)
Water
Honey (to taste)

Place the dried nettle leaves into a tea pot and pour over the boiling water (for each 1 tablespoon of leaves add 1 cup of boiling water). Place the lid on the teapot and a tea cosy and allow to steep for 10 minutes. To serve hot, strain the tea into a cup and add the honey to taste. Or, strain the tea into a jug and allow to cool before placing in the fridge and serve cold with a dollop of honey and slice of lemon.

Wild Summer Salad

A delightful accompaniment to a summer BBQ…

½ salad bowl seasonal flowers *(try a mixture of black mustard, sea radish, mallow, evening primrose, ribwort plantain, borage, rock samphire, dandelion, wild thyme, clover)*
½ salad bowl seasonal leaves *(try a mixture of dandelion, plantain, black mustard, tree mallow, violet, daisy, dead nettle, yarrow, marjoram, fennel, garlic, sorrel)*
Salad dressing *(of your choice)*
Salt to taste

Wash the leaves to remove any bugs and shred. Gently wash the flowers again, checking for bugs and dry gently. Add the leaves and flowers to a salad bowl and fold in your favourite dressing.

Elderflower Bread

Delicious served warm for afternoon tea...

1 lb. wholemeal flour	**½ pt. warm water**
1 tsp. quick yeast	**4 fl. oz. elderflower cordial**
Pinch of salt	**1 tbsp. of olive oil**

Add the flour, salt and quick yeast into a large mixing bowl and stir. Next, slowly add the warm water, elderflower cordial and oil to the flour mix and knead for 15 minutes. Place the dough in a greased 1 lb. loaf tin, cover with a clean cloth and leave in a warm place for 20 minutes. Remove the cloth and bake in a preheated oven at Gas 6/200°C for 40-45minutes.

Wild Herb Butter Bread

A wild change from garlic bread…

Handful wild herbs
(try a selection of wild celery, sorrel, wild chervil, sage, rosemary, wild garlic, or marjoram)
1 lb. of butter
1 baguette

Bring the butter to room temperature. Chop the herbs finely and mix together in a bowl with butter. Slice the baguette across-ways but ensuring you do not cut all the way through and butter each slice. The remaining butter will keep in the fridge for a week or so. Wrap the baguette in foil and bake in a hot oven (Gas 6/200C°) for 15 minutes. Serve warm.

METRIC CONVERSIONS

The weights, measures and oven temperatures used in the preceding recipes can be easily converted to their metric equivalents. The conversions listed below are only approximate, having been rounded up or down as may be appropriate.

Weights

Avoirdupois	Metric
1 oz.	just under 30 grams
4 oz. (¼ lb.)	app. 115 grams
8 oz. (½ lb.)	app. 230 grams
1 lb.	454 grams

Liquid Measures

Imperial	Metric
1 tablespoon (liquid only)	20 millilitres
1 fl. oz.	app. 30 millilitres
1 gill (¼ pt.)	app. 145 millilitres
½ pt.	app. 285 millilitres
1 pt.	app. 570 millilitres
1 qt.	app. 1.140 litres

Oven Temperatures

	°Fahrenheit	Gas Mark	°Celsius
Slow	300	2	150
	325	3	170
Moderate	350	4	180
	375	5	190
	400	6	200
Hot	425	7	220
	450	8	230
	475	9	240

Flour as specified in these recipes refers to plain flour unless otherwise described.